Do It Yourself Projects!

Make Your Own
Books

Anna-Marie D'Cruz

PowerKiDS press
New York

Published in 2009 by
The Rosen Publishing Group Inc.
29 East 21st Street,
New York, NY 10010

First Edition

Senior Editor: Jennifer Schofield
Designer: Jason Billin
Project maker: Anna-Marie D'Cruz
Photographer: Chris Fairclough
Proofreader: Susie Brooks

Library of Congress Cataloging-in-Publication Data

D'Cruz, Anna-Marie.
   Make your own books / Anna-Marie D'Cruz. — 1st ed.
      p. cm. — (Do it yourself projects)
   Includes index.
   ISBN 978-1-4358-2855-1 (library binding)
   ISBN 978-1-4358-2927-5 (paperback)
   ISBN 978-1-4358-2928-2 (6-pack)
   1. Book design—Juvenile literature. 2. Bookbinding—Juvenile
   literature. 3. Books—Juvenile literature. I. Title.
   Z246.D43 2009
   686—dc22
                                        2008033659

Manufactured in China

Acknowledgments
The Publishers would like to thank the following models:
Emel Augustin, Jade Campbell, Ammar Duffus, Akash Kohli,
Ellie Lawrence, Katie Powell, Eloise Ramplin, Robin Stevens

Picture Credits:
All photography by Chris Fairclough except for page 4 top
Brooklyn Museum/CORBIS; Page 4 bottom CORBIS; page 7
Bob Krist/CORBIS;

Note to parents and teachers:
The projects in this book are designed to be made by children. However, we do recommend adult supervision at all times since the Publisher cannot be held responsible for any injury caused while making the projects.

Contents

All about books

We read and use books all the time, from storybooks and notebooks, to address books and telephone directories. But books as we know them have changed a lot since they were first made.

BOOKS AND WRITING

Books are linked to the start of writing. As long ago as 10,000 BCE in China and the Middle East, people wrote things down on clay and later on wax. In about 2500 BCE, the Ancient Egyptians used papyrus to make a type of paper (see right). Papyrus is a reed that grows next to water. The leaves of the plant were pressed and dried to make the papyrus, which could be used like a piece of paper.

Today's books are all printed on huge printing presses, but this has not always been the case. In about 700 CE, the Chinese invented a type of printing—woodblock printing. They carved out letters from blocks of wood and then covered them with ink. The inked blocks were then pressed down on paper—similar to using a stamp—so that the letters were printed on the page. A major change in printing took place in about 1438, when Germany's Johannes Gutenberg invented the printing press. In 1455, Gutenberg used his press to print a Bible (see left).

TODAY'S BOOKS

Books come in all kinds of different styles, sizes, and shapes. The process of putting a book together is known as bookbinding. Books can be bound in different ways— for example, the pages can be stitched or stapled to keep them together, or they can be glued. Books usually have a cover to protect the inside pages. The covers need to be strong and are often made from materials such as cardboard, wood, and leather.

Books can be used for many different things. They can provide information, such as an encyclopedia, dictionary, or atlas, or they can be used to keep records of things, as in an address book or a notebook.

GET STARTED!

In this book, there are projects for creating many different kinds of book. When you make your books, try to use materials that you already have, either at home or at school. For example, instead of buying cardboard, the backs of used notepads, writing pads, art pads, and hardbacked envelopes are ideal. Reusing and recycling materials like this is good for the environment and it saves you money. The projects have all been made and decorated for this book, but do not worry if yours look a little different—just have fun making them.

Button holder

Fabric is great for making books, because it is strong and can be washed. In this project, you can make your own fabric book for keeping your favorite buttons safe.

YOU WILL NEED

3 different-colored
  pieces of felt
pair of scissors
stapler
2 pieces of ribbon,
  16 in. (40cm) long
craft glue

1 Cut one large, one medium, and one small rectangle from the felt. If you have a pair of pinking shears, then use these instead of scissors to give a zigzag effect.

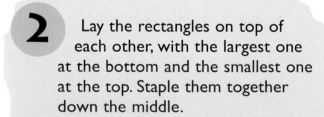

2 Lay the rectangles on top of each other, with the largest one at the bottom and the smallest one at the top. Staple them together down the middle.

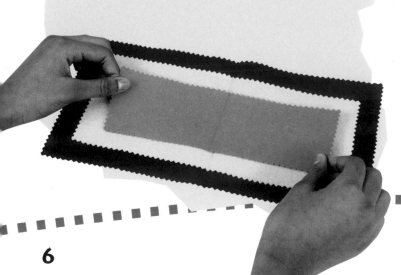

3 Fold the end of one piece of ribbon over, and staple it halfway up the side of the front cover of the book. Do the same with the other piece of ribbon, this time stapling it to the back cover. Be careful not to staple the pages together.

4 To decorate the front cover, cut out and glue on shapes of felt.

FABULOUS FELT

Felt is a fabric made from wool. This means that it is good for making hats and clothes that keep you warm. It is used in Mongolia, where it is extremely cold, to make tents known as yurts.

5 You can now start pinning your buttons to the felt pages to keep your collection safe.

Folding book

Folding books were first used in Thailand and Myanmar. They were made from long sheets of paper that were folded into zigzag shapes. Follow these steps to make your own folding book. If you like, you can decorate it with symbols of the Chinese zodiac.

YOU WILL NEED

sheet of red card

ruler

pencil

pair of scissors

glue

colored foam sheet

square of corrugated cardboard, 3½ x 3½ in. (9 x 9cm)

newspaper

paint and paintbrush

green card, 2 3½ x 3½ in. (9 x 9cm)

2 squares of stiff card, 3½ x 3½ in. (9 x 9cm)

12 squares of yellow paper, 2 x 2 in. (5 x 5cm)

colored pencils

rubber band

1 Measure and cut three strips of red card that are 2¾ in. (7cm) wide and the length of the card. Glue the strips together, overlapping each end by ⅝ in. (1.5cm), to make one long strip.

2 Fold one end of the strip of card over by 2¾ in. (7cm). Then fold it back the other way, also by 2¾ in. (7cm). Continue folding backward and forward to create a zigzag. Trim off any extra card.

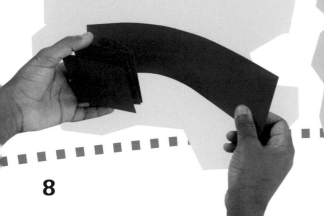

3 To make a stamp to decorate the book's cover, cut out a shape from the foam sheet—we have used a Chinese symbol. Flip the shape over so that it is reversed. Then glue the shape to the square of corrugated cardboard.

4 Cover your work surface with newspaper. To make the book covers, brush paint on the stamp and press it onto one of the green squares of card. Repeat the print on the other green square. Glue the green squares onto the squares of stiff card.

5 Glue the back of one of the covers to the end of the red zigzag. Fold up the zigzag and glue the second cover to the other end. Make sure your cover is the correct way up!

6 On the twelve yellow squares, draw pictures or write a story. Glue one of the yellow squares on each page.

CHINESE ZODIAC

In China, each year is symbolized by a different animal. These are the rat, bull, tiger, rabbit, dragon, snake, horse, sheep, monkey, rooster, dog, and pig. Try to find out which animal represents the year in which you were born.

7 When the glue has dried, close the book and place a rubber band around it to hold it closed.

Palm-leaf book

Palm-leaf books get their name because their pages were traditionally made from the leaves of palm trees. The books had wooden covers to protect their pages. Make your own palm-leaf-style book and use it to record your favorite recipe.

1 To make the pages, mark ten strips that are 8¼ x ¾ in. (21 x 2cm) on the green card. Cut them out.

YOU WILL NEED

sheet of green card
ruler
pen or pencil
pair of scissors
hole punch
sheet of black card
glue
metallic pens
40 in. (1m) of cord
2 beads that will thread on the cord

2 Measure 4¼ in. (10.5cm) from the edge of each strip and make a mark. Use this to position a hole punch so that the holes will be in the same place on each strip. Punch holes in the card.

3 For the covers, cut two rectangles measuring 8¼ x 1½ in. (21 x 4cm) from the black card. Fold each one in half along the length, and glue the insides together. Punch holes in the same position as in the green strips. Use the metallic pens to decorate each cover.

4 Thread the cord ends through the holes on the decorated side of one cover. Then thread the pages on one by one, finishing with the other cover, with the decorated side on the outside.

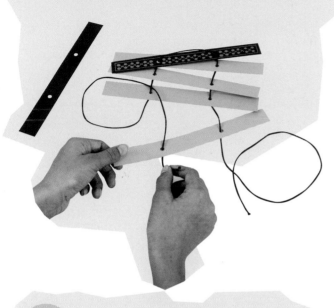

5 Tie a double knot about 4 in. (10cm) in from the end of each cord. Thread on a bead and tie a knot just above it.

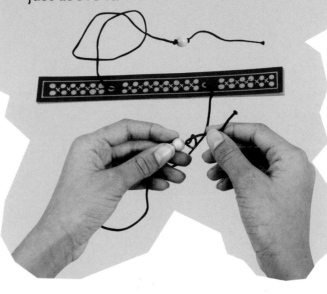

6 Spread the "leaves" and write down your recipe. Then gather the pages together and tie the cord around them for safe keeping.

Scrambled eggs

Ingredients: 2 eggs, 1 tbs milk, salt, pepper, knob of butter, toast to serve

Method: 1. Whisk together the eggs, milk, salt, and pepper.

2. Melt the butter in a frying pan until it starts to bubble.

3. Add the egg mixture and stir

RECIPES

A recipe is a set of instructions explaining how to cook something. Recipes have a list of what you need (the ingredients) and a set of instructions telling you how to prepare the dish.

Lift the flaps

In a lift-the-flap book, hidden areas on the pages are discovered by lifting a piece of paper. Why not write your own story for a lift-the-flap book?

YOU WILL NEED

several sheets of white paper

pens

pencil

sheets of colored card

pair of scissors

glue

felt-tip pens

stapler

1 Think about a story. Write it down on some paper.

2 Plan the pictures for your story—lift-the flap books work best with pictures where something is hiding or is inside something else. What do you want the flap to be hiding? This will need to be part of the main picture.

3 When you are happy with your story, draw the main picture on one half of a clean sheet of white paper. The object being hidden needs to be part of this drawing.

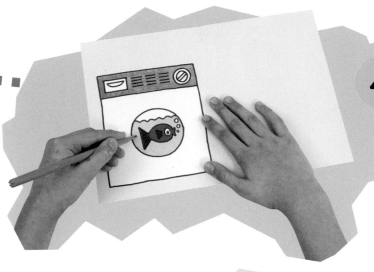

4 Fold a sheet of colored card in half. Cut out and paste the main picture onto one half of the card. Color it in.

5 On another sheet of paper, make the flap by drawing the front of the hiding place. Color it in and cut it out. Glue your flap onto the main drawing.

6 Repeat steps one to five until you have drawn pictures for the whole story. Glue every two pages back to back, and staple all the pages together when you are finished to make a book.

Pop-up book

A pop-up book is always full of surprises. Each time you turn a page, something will spring out at you. Follow these steps to make a simple pop-up.

YOU WILL NEED

sheets of colored card
permanent marker
ruler
pencil
pair of scissors
colored pencils
glue

1 Fold a sheet of colored card in half. Draw two horizontal lines from the folded edge that are 2 in. (5cm) long.

2 Cut along the lines. Bend back the middle section, as shown.

3 Open up your card and push the cut shape inward. Close your card and press it flat. Open the card again, so that you have a pop-up rectangle.

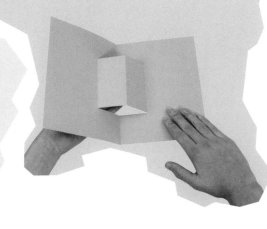

4 Measure the width of your card, from the fold to the edge. This will tell you how wide your pop-up picture can be. If it is any wider, then your picture will stick out of the side when the page is closed.

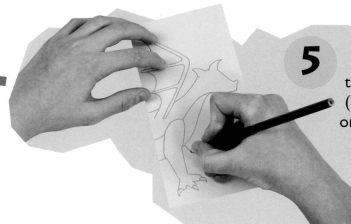

5 Cut another piece of card as wide as the measurement from step 4 and 8¼ in. (21cm) high. Draw what you want to be on your pop-up on this card.

6 Color in the drawing, cut it out, and glue it to the pop-up rectangle. You could make more than one pop-up on the same-sized card and glue each one together. Write your story below the pictures.

MORE POP-UPS

The shape of the pop-up can vary, as shown below. Experiment with different shapes by changing the way you make the cut in steps 1 and 2.

Address book

To make an alphabetical address book, you need to use tabs. The tabs allow you to quickly turn to the pages you want. Put a hardback cover on your book to protect the pages.

YOU WILL NEED

8 sheets of paper

stapler

pencil

ruler

pair of scissors

eraser

2 pieces of card,
6 x 8½ in. (15 x 22cm)

1 strip of card,
¼ x 8½ in. (0.5 x 22cm)

sheet of wrapping paper,
14¼ x 10¼ in.
(36 x 26cm)

glue

pen

1 Fold all your sheets of paper in half to make a crease. Unfold the paper, and keeping the pages together, staple down the crease and fold.

2 To make the tabs, use a pencil and ruler to draw a line down the right-hand side of the third page, about ¾ in. (2cm) in from the edge. Lightly mark 13 equal lengths, each about ⅝ in. (1.5cm), on this line.

3 Cut the third page from the bottom up to the top mark, to leave a tab at the top. Cut the next page up to the second mark so that it appears beneath the top tab. Do the same for each sheet, each time cutting up to the next mark down, until you end up with 13 tabs. Erase any pencil marks.

4 To add the cover, glue the card shapes onto the back of the wrapping paper, as shown. The gap between the spine and covers needs to be at least ¼ in. (0.5cm).

5 Glue and fold over the top and bottom. Then glue and fold in the sides, pressing down firmly.

6 Take your tabbed pages and put glue on the front page. Glue this to the center of the inside front cover. Put glue on the back page and stick it down.

7 Write the alphabet in pairs of letters down the side on the tabs. The address book is now ready to use.

EF
GH
IJ
KL
MN
OP
QR
ST
UV
WX
YZ

Photo album

A photo album is a book for displaying photographs and keeping them safe. Make your own album to hold your favorite family photographs. You could decorate the cover with your family tree.

YOU WILL NEED

5 sheets of colored paper
pair of scissors
5 sheets of tracing paper
sheet of colored card
8¼ x 6 in. (21 x 15cm) reused card
9 x 6 in. (23 x 15cm) reused card
glue
hole punch
colored paper for decorating
2 paper fasteners

1 Cut the 5 sheets of colored paper in half across the width to give you 10 sheets. Do the same with the tracing paper.

2 Cut the sheet of colored card in half, and glue it onto the two rectangles of reused card to hide any writing or pictures. On the longer cover, not all of the print or pictures will be hidden.

3 Punch holes in all the sheets of paper and in the covers, in the middle of one of the short edges. Make sure the holes are in the same place on each page. For the longer cover, the holes should be along the uncovered edge. Fold the covers on the holed side about ¾ in. (2cm) in from the edge.

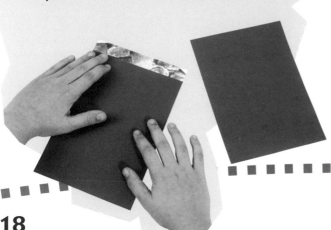

4 Turn the shorter cover over and decorate it. You could cut out a tree trunk and branch shape from colored paper and glue them down. Cut circles of card and glue them down to the ends of the branches. Write the names of people in your family on the circles.

5 To bind the photo album together, put the front cover face down, placing the holes over two unopened paper fasteners. Take turns placing a sheet of tracing paper and then colored paper over the fasteners.

6 Place the longer cover over the fasteners, sticking out the opposite way from the pile of pages. Make sure the colored card is facing downward. Open up the fasteners, and fold the card over the book to finish the back cover.

7 Your album is now ready for photographs. You can add more sheets if you need to by removing the back cover.

FAMILY TREES

A family tree is a chart showing how different members of a family are connected. They can also give information of when people were born and died, where they lived, and what they did for work. They can tell you a lot about your family history.

Eco-notebook

Making your own paper is a great way to recycle pieces of old newspaper. Put together sheets of handmade paper to make an environmentally friendly notebook.

YOU WILL NEED

4 long popsicle sticks

4 rubber bands

pair of clean, old tights

pair of scissors

newspaper torn into small pieces plus 1 extra newspaper

plastic wash basin

5 pints of warm tap water

balloon whisk

2 old facecloths

rolling pin

hole punch

string

1 To make a frame, lay the popsicle sticks in a square shape and wrap the rubber bands tightly around the corners. You will need a frame for each sheet of paper you make.

2 Cut off a piece from a leg of the tights, and pull it over the frame to make a screen.

3 Put the torn pieces of newspaper into the wash basin with the warm water. Allow the paper to soak for about three hours. Then use the whisk to mash up the paper. Keep resting the mixture and whisking again, until you have a gray "pulp" that looks like thick soup. This may take a while, so be patient!

4 For a blotting surface, lay half of the extra newspaper down and place one of the facecloths on top. Keep the rest of the newspaper and the other facecloth nearby.

REED PAPER

The Ancient Egyptians made a type of paper called papyrus. It was made from pieces of the papyrus reed that were placed side by side, and then another layer was put on top at right angles. The papyrus was then soaked, squeezed dry, and hammered to flatten it into a thin sheet of "paper."

5 Slide the frame into the basin, wriggling it around to get an even layer of pulp on your screen. Pull up the frame, keeping it as level as possible. Allow the water to drip through into the basin. Lay the frame on the blotting surface.

6 Cover the frame with the other facecloth. Put the remaining newspaper over the cloth. Use the rolling pin to squeeze out as much water as possible.

7 Lift up the top part of the blotter. Lift off the frame and allow it to dry. When it is dry, carefully peel off the paper. Repeat steps four to seven to make more paper. Trim the pages to neaten them up. Punch a hole in the paper, in the same place on each sheet, and tie the pages together with string to make a notebook.

Glossary

alphabetical

When something is in the order of the alphabet—from A to Z.

binding

The way the pages in a book are held together. Some books are stitched down the middle, and others are stapled or glued.

blotter

Something that soaks up water or other liquids.

Chinese Zodiac

The twelve animals that represent different years in the Chinese calendar.

environmentally friendly

When something is good for the environment or will not damage the Earth, it is environmentally friendly. Reusing and recycling are environmentally friendly.

felt

A thick type of fabric made from wool.

material

Anything used for making something else. Wool, wood, plastic, and metal are all materials.

Middle East

The countries to the east of the Mediterranean Sea. The Middle East includes Egypt, Iraq, and Iran.

Mongolia

A country in central Asia.

papyrus

A water plant that was used to make a type of paper in Ancient Egypt.

pinking shears

A special kind of scissors that cut zigzags instead of straight lines.

printing press

A machine that can print thousands of copies of a document at once.

recipe

A set of instructions for cooking a particular dish of food. Recipes usually list the ingredients of the dish, and then tell you what to do to prepare the food and in what order to do it.

recycling

To recycle something is to change it or treat it so that it can be used again.

reusing

Using something for a different purpose. For example, if you use the cardboard from a cereal box to make a project, you are reusing the cardboard.

right angle

An angle of 90 degrees. The corners of a rectangle and square are angled at 90 degrees.

tab

A small strip or flap that sticks out. Sometimes tabs are labeled with numbers or letters, depending on the information they store.

woodblock printing

A method of printing that started in China in about 700 CE. Letters were carved into wood and "stamped" on paper.

yurts

A circle-shaped tent used by the nomads (people who move their homes around) of Mongolia.

FURTHER INFORMATION

BOOKS TO READ

DIY Kids
by Ellen Lupton and Julia Lupton
(Princeton Architectural Press, 2007)

The Book Book: A Journey into Bookmaking
by Sophie Benini Pietromarchi
(Tara Publishing, 2007)

WEB SITES

Due to the changing nature of Internet links, PowerKids Press has developed an online list of Web sites related to the subject of this book. This site is updated regularly. Please use this link to access this list:
www.powerkidslinks.com/diyp/books

Index

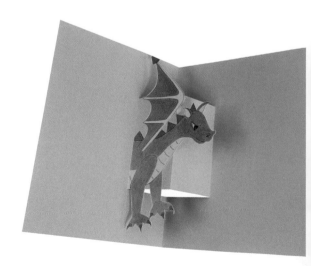